Summer Surprise

by Mary Jo Huff

illustrated by Jerry Jindrich

DEDICATION

During my 30 wonderful years of being involved with educators across this great country, I have experienced life from one season to another.

Each person who has played in one of my workshops, attended a performance, sent me a note, called on the phone or e-mailed me has a special place in my storytelling heart. Dr. Jean Feldman, Drs. Sue and Ralph Unger, Teresa Fogarty, Dr. Thomas Moore, Maria Elena Buria, Lisa Hoover and all my on the road friends, have influenced and supported my many endeavors

My praises and gratitude go out to every person who encourages children to use language and tell their story. Youth storytelling in the United States is on a new path and we should all encourage this movement.

Publisher: Roberta Suid

Production: Little Acorn & Associates, Inc.

SUMMER SURPRISE
Entire contents copyright © 2003
by Monday Morning Books, Inc.

For a complete catalog, write to the address below:
Monday Morning Books, Inc.
PO Box 1134
Inverness, CA 94937

Call our toll-free number: 1-800-255-6049
E-mail us at: MMBooks@aol.com
Visit our Web site:
http://www.mondaymorningbooks.com

Monday Morning is a registered trademark of
Monday Morning Books, Inc.

ISBN 1-57612-182-8

Printed in the United States of America
9 8 7 6 5 4 3 2 1

Contents

Introduction

The seasons come and the seasons go but summer seems to stay longer. When the warm breezes blow across the land people everywhere celebrate the leisure of life. Wild animals in the bush or in the zoo romp and play in the sun. The oceans are filled with activity from all species.

The *Summer Surprise* book will delight storytellers and story listeners. It is part of a complete season series including *Winter Whimsy*, *Fall Frolic*, and *Spring Fling*.

This collection of rhymes and puppets can be used with many different stories. Use your imagination and adapt the puppets to many stories and let the children use puppets to retell a story.

Provide children with puppets to enhance a story. This interactive story connection promotes attention and memory development. When children make up their own stories they are thinking creatively. Sing songs and use puppets to reinforce language and speech development.

Using puppets from different countries can create a multicultural awareness for children. Themes, units, creative curriculum or any method you use in your setting can adapt to the use of puppets.

Dramatic play can be enhanced with puppets from different countries. Using the puppets with shoe box scenery or stand up scenery, that the children create, is a good independent or small group activity. Group activities give children a sense of cooperation.

When children need quiet time, encourage them to interact with a puppet instead of using the time-out method. Let the child have a few minutes in a place where he or she might interact with a puppet. This can be nurturing and relaxing and decrease hyperactivity.

Ask children who are ready to read to a puppet. The puppet becomes their reading partner. Using a finger puppet can encourage children to follow the text, and they may find it easier to complete and enjoy this type of task.

Puppet fun can become an exciting time in the day. Encourage children to reach into a puppet bag and feel for a puppet they would like to use. Ask children to describe the puppet they are feeling and guess what character the puppet may be.

Questions to ask the child:

- What is it?
- What color is the puppet?
- Where does this puppet live?
- What sound does this puppet make?
- Does this puppet like warm or cold weather?

Investigate, create and motivate your class with the simplicity of a class mascot. Small children are believers in talking puppets and older children can become the talker for the puppet.

Family Fun is a connection between the classroom and the home. Children are encouraged to take home ideas and projects that extend the learning process. Ideas are provided to help teachers with this connection. Provide adequate information for the children and parents to interact with language, science, math and literacy projects.

Word Play

Pick out words from a story that are important to your curriculum. Choose enough words for each student in the class. Print or type the words on a card and place them in a story basket.

Invite a puppet to choose a word and then pronounce the word. Ask a child to use the word in a sentence. The child will enjoy interacting with the puppet and sharing language.

The sentence is the beginning of a story. Each child then takes a word out of the story basket and adds a sentence to the story. Write the sentences on a wipe-off board or word wall. The puppet can help pronounce and prompt children when doing this word play.

Tape the story and let the children listen to a retelling. After doing this word play several times, the children get quicker and sharper. They especially enjoy listening to the retelling.

Perfect partner
Unique
Playful
Persuasive
Educator
Tool

Puppet Stuff

The following is a list of items to save for future puppet making. Store your items in clear shoe box containers and label them for easy use. When you get hooked on making puppets to accompany your storytelling you will see puppets in things you would have thrown away before this experience.

Share this list with friends, parents and relatives and you will be amazed at how helpful they will become in your puppet endeavor. Ask them to save their throw-away items.

Jugs	Sponges	Mops
Shoe Boxes	Fake Fur	Wire Coat Hangers
Buttons	Paper Plates	Cups
Material	Bags	Newspapers
Egg Cartons	Rubberbands	Twister Ties
Straws	Dowel Rods	Felt
Ping Pong Balls	Panty Hose	
Cardboard Tubes	Tennis Balls	
Socks	Spoons	

The items are but a few of the many you will find and use to create puppets to accompany your stories.

Storage

Purchase clear containers from your local discount store. Make labels for each box and add items to the box as they are donated or purchased. Organizing the items is a big step in learning how to use multiple items when making puppets. This also teaches children about organizing. They need to be responsible for returning items to their proper container.

The power and magic of a puppet is not in the construction—but in its use! Not the product but the process!!!

Puppet Stuff

Puppet See–Puppet Do

Puppets can do anything you can do! Puppets can teach just like you. They can read, perform science experiments and act as a class leader. You do not have to be a professional puppeteer to become effective for children. Just use a puppet to help you expand oral language experiences for the children and enhance the creativity within your classroom. Puppets can become part of the teaching/learning process.

Puppets should not become theatrical entertainment but an integral part of the curriculum. Use puppets in the classroom or at home to teach language, science, music, drama, mathematics, social studies, social skills and nutrition.

What Can A Puppet Do?

Puppets can help children:
- Understand the written word through stories
- Develop an ability to communicate with others
- Practice good listening skills
- Develop language skills
- Form an appreciation of good literature
- Communicate ideas and information
- Learn how to work cooperatively in groups
- Improve critical thinking skills
- Emphasize thinking processes and concept development
- Reinforce new language and written symbols
- Communicate through dramatization
- Express emotions and inner feelings

Puppet Stuff

Story Puppetry

Find a story with one or two main characters so you can use your hands to hold the puppet. If a story has many characters, let the children act out the smaller parts.

Puppets are magic and the audience will focus on the puppet not the puppeteer. Find a comfort zone with your chosen puppet and story. The puppet does not have to tell the story. It can introduce the story and interject throughout the telling of a good story. As the story is retold several times, you may find yourself letting the puppet tell more and more of the story.

Puppet Voices

Feel the character in your puppet and find a voice that fits your style while you interact with your newfound friend. Talk to and with the puppet so you become comfortable hearing your own voice and the voice you use for the puppet.

Puppet Etiquette

Puppets should never be allowed to fight. Set limits for puppet activity and treat all puppets with respect. The children will model your behavior. Remind the children that puppets never hit, puppets never fight and puppets never bite. Puppets can be silly, smart, brave, shy, aggressive, goofy, happy, sad or any other personality you choose. When using different personalities with puppets such as a crying puppet—cry loud, as if tears are flowing from your eyes. Make your character believable.

Puppet Characters

Each puppet has a special personality. Be consistent when you decide on the exact personality. Give the puppet a name, family, mannerisms, voice, age and a connection with your environment. Practice until you feel comfortable and then watch the children as they become familiar with all aspects of your puppet's character.

Puppet Stuff

Puppet Talk

Puppets do not have to be used to tell a story. They can talk about the story and introduce the setting, characters or plot. They can get excited about what the children are going to listen to and this sets the stage for good storytelling.

Puppet Movements

- Walking – slow and fast
- Running – forward and in circles
- Climbing – climbing up and down
- Turning – looking in a different direction or focusing on a particular item
- Jumping – children can jump with the puppet
- Falling – children laugh when a puppet falls down
- Dancing – let the puppet dance to music

Puppet Hints

Focus – do not focus on the audience but on the puppet that is an extension of your hand. The audience will then focus on the puppet and not the puppeteer.

Mouth Movement

Practice opening the mouth on the important words and syllables. Practice the method of swooping and opening. Do not open the mouth wide and let the eyes disappear. Be comfortable and find a natural way to use the puppet.

Practice

Practice these methods and voices while spending time in your car. Put on some good music or practice a monologue using different voices. You soon will become comfortable with your choice for a specific puppet.

Throughout this book you will find many different puppets. Use your imagination. Create puppets from materials you have available and always be on the watch for new and creative ideas.

Puppet Stuff

Language Development

When children use puppets to retell a story they are developing their language skills. Make puppets accessible to children. I always suggest finding a special place in a story area for children to retell stories. Give the puppets a special place to live and create puppet houses. Do not let children mistreat puppets! When they have a special house, the children are responsible for caring for each puppet and putting them in their respective houses when puppet and story play are finished.

Puppet Houses

Puppet houses can be created out of almost anything. A few suggestions are copy paper boxes, shoe boxes, coffee cans (all sizes), ice cream buckets and picnic baskets. Invite the children to paint and decorate a box for their puppets. They will take ownership in their creation and it reinforces the child's responsibility.

Creating a puppet encourages children and teachers to add items to the house that are part of the curriculum. The puppet and his house become an integral part of the classroom setting and will open up many doors for conversation.

This type of activity encourages the interaction of the children and the puppets. There is no end to the possibilities of creating special places for puppets to live.

My Summer Story

In the summer I like to _____ .

In the summer I like to eat _____ .

My favorite thing about summer is _____

_____ .

This is me in the summer.

Kid Fun

The children can fill in the blanks and this story can be sent home for the family to read.

Family Fun

The family can take this beginning and write their own summer story.

Mascot

I encourage you to find a special puppet for a mascot. The puppet should have an opening that fits your hand. Be comfortable manipulating the puppet. Prepare to use the puppet in your year-round seasonal curriculum.

A mascot can be active in every aspect of the curriculum. Think how you could put a puppet to use every day. Let your mascot puppet:

- Do a morning greeting
- Say hello in different languages
- Do the weather report
- Write notes to the teacher or children
- Explain the daily activities
- Introduce visitors
- Smile, deliver good messages, read
- Attend field trips
- Visit other classes

A mascot can also visit with parents at an open house or special time when the parents visit. A puppet can convey many messages that may be troublesome for you. They can express the importance of parent involvement with their children.

On a special reading night, the mascot puppet can read to the children and adults. Even adults relate to the messages from the puppet and will laugh and sing with the mascot.

The mascot can go along on field trips and carry a first aid kit in a backpack. He can be the rule setter and leader on the trip.

The puppet can wear a costume from other countries and become a global connection to other areas of our world.

Spend some time deciding on the mascot puppet that will fit into your curriculum. Look around your community and document what the puppet can bring to the classroom from the community. Invite the puppet mascot to go on trips with you around the community and then document what you and the puppet say to the children about your adventures.

Mascot

Summer Connection

Dress the mascot in summer clothes; prepare his house with a summer decor. The mascot can go on a summer vacation. Talk and document the mascot's vacation.

Spread a beach towel on the floor, bring in some sand, add a sand bucket, a snorkel, fish milk jugs and any other items that you have available to create a summer atmosphere.

Talk about summer safety on the beach, riding your bike, going to the park and attending a picnic. Invite other creatures into your puppet's life. Pick creatures that the puppet might visit in the summer.

Smile Fun

Look at rhymes and stories to see if you can add a puppet to the experience of interacting with the words. The following is an example of a simple stick puppet and a little rhyme.

CHANT (chant to the rhythm of B I N G O)
–spell the word S M I L E = (refrain)

S M I L E
S M I L E
S M I L E

Smiling, Smiling, Smiling

Smiling is a lot of fun.
It flows from me to you.
When I smiled at someone else today.
They started smiling, too.

Repeat S M I L E Refrain

I looked around at all my friends
And someone saw my grin.
He/She smiled at me and then I knew.
I'd passed it onto them.

Repeat S M I L E Refrain

I smiled at him/her; he/she smiled at me
We shared some fun right then.
Open up the world to all
And let your smiles begin.

Repeat S M I L E Refrain

Smile Puppet

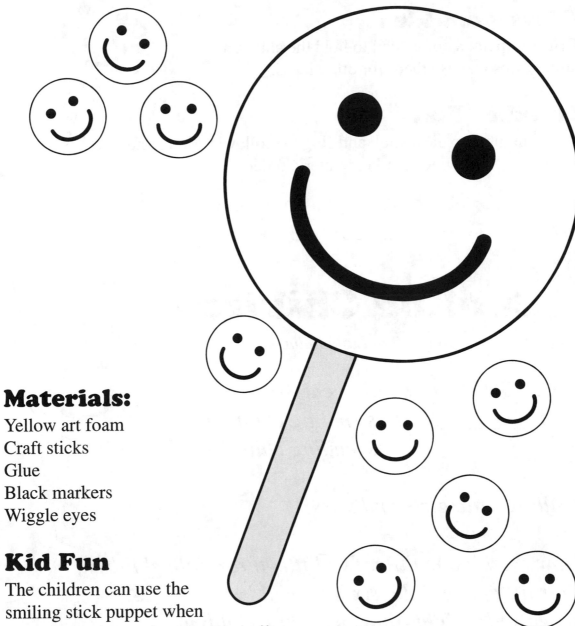

Materials:

Yellow art foam
Craft sticks
Glue
Black markers
Wiggle eyes

Kid Fun

The children can use the smiling stick puppet when they chant, sing and repeat the smile message.

Family Fun

The family can each create a smile puppet and chant, sing and repeat the smile message many, many times. They can share it with other members of their extended family and the world will share more smiles.

Classroom Idea

Cover or paint a coffee can to hold the children's smile faces and use them for other ideas.

Number Fun

Add a number to each stick and sing the following song and invite the children to stand in numeric order.

Smiling Children

(Sing to *Ten Little Indians*.)

Mrs. JONES has smiling children
Mrs. _____ has smiling children
Mrs. _____ has smiling children

Smiling little girls and boys!

Now there's one little, two little, three little children,
four little, five little, six little children,
seven little, eight little, nine little children,
Ten little smiling children

(According to your class number –add eleven little, twelve little, thirteen little, fourteen little etc. for the last line.)

Smile Puppet Pattern

Weather Watcher

It is a Monday.
Monday Sunshine *(arms in a circle over head)*
All you Weather Watchers
It's OK.

It is a Tuesday.
Tuesday Clouds *(float hands above head)*
Monday Sunshine
All you Weather Watchers
It's OK.

It is a Wednesday. *(clap hands)*
Wednesday Thunder
Tuesday Clouds
Monday Sunshine
All you Weather Watchers
It's OK.

It is a Thursday.
Thursday Lightning *(use hand to streak in the air)*
Wednesday Thunder
Tuesday Clouds
Monday Sunshine
All you Weather Watchers
It's OK.

Weather Watcher

It is a Friday.
Friday Wind *(blow between hands)*
Thursday Lightning
Wednesday Thunder
Tuesday Clouds
Monday Sunshine
All you Weather Watchers
It's OK.

It is a Saturday.
Saturday Rain *(fingers make rain)*
Friday Wind
Thursday Lightning
Wednesday Thunder
Tuesday Clouds
Monday Sunshine
All you Weather Watchers
It's OK.

Weather Watcher

It is a Sunday.
Sunday Rainbows *(use arms to make rainbow arch)*
Saturday Rain
Friday Wind
Thursday Lightning
Wednesday Thunder
Tuesday Clouds
Monday Sunshine
All you Weather Watchers
It's OK!

Extended Classroom Activity

Find weather pictures in magazines or from posters and attach to a piece of poster board with the weekday word printed on the bottom in large letters. This activity is one that can be repeated over and over again in the classroom.

This activity creates an interactive awareness of the days of the week. The children become daily Weather Watchers!

Summer Surprise © 2003 Monday Morning Books, Inc.

Ant and Grasshopper

One day in a time before yesterday, there was a small ant who knew it was time to plant her garden. The little ant worked the ground with her tiny little feet and planted some seeds in the warm soft, sifted dirt. She covered the seeds and the sun and the rain helped the plants grow.

While the little ant was working so hard, the grasshopper was spending his days singing, playing and watching the ant work. The grasshopper jumped around and around the little ant singing his songs of spring. He invited the ant to join him but the ant knew how much work needed to be done.

The ant told the grasshopper he should be thinking about doing some work because winter would soon be upon them. The grasshopper just laughed and said, "It is spring and time to dance and sing."

Work, Work All Day Long
Said the Little Ant
This Is My Song!

Dance and Play All Day Long
Said the Little Grasshopper
This Is My Song!

On a hot summer day, ant was busy working in her garden. She was pulling weeds and loosening the dirt around her growing plants. The sun was hot, the wind was blowing and rain was on the way. Grasshopper was fooling around and resting in the shade of the big tree. He said, "Ant, you do not have to work so hard; come and join me in the shade of this big tree."

Ant and Grasshopper

Work, Work All Day Long
Said the Little Ant
This Is My Song!

Dance and Play All Day Long
Said the Little Grasshopper
This Is My Song!

Ant again told grasshopper he should be thinking about doing some work because winter was getting closer. Grasshopper told ant it was summer and he did not want to think about winter. He said, "Summer is too much fun to think about the cold winter."

One brisk fall day, the ant was busy taking in the harvest from the garden. She was taking the vegetables and fruits to her home in preparation for winter. Grasshopper was busy dancing and singing in the colorful fallen leaves. "Come join me in some fun little ant; you are working too hard" said the grasshopper. "I have to get my garden work done because winter is getting closer every day. You need to think about winter," said the little ant.

Work, Work All Day Long
Said the Little Ant
This Is My Song!

Dance and Play All Day Long
Said the Little Grasshopper
This Is My Song!

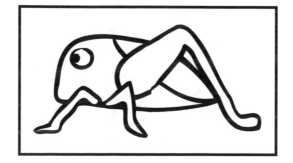

Ant and Grasshopper

Winter arrived and brought cold winds and icy rain. The grasshopper could only find little bits of grass and he shivered from the cold. Then it snowed and grasshopper could not find any grass to eat. He was so hungry and cold. He went to ant's house and knocked on the door. When ant came to the door grasshopper asked if he could come in and get warm and get something to eat.

The ant said, "Why, aren't you dancing and singing now? In the spring you made fun of me, in the summer you slept under the big shade tree and in the fall you spent your time dancing and singing in the fallen leaves, while I worked in my garden." "You are right ant. I was foolish and should have been concerned about winter. I promise to help you next spring if you will just let me come in and stay."

The ant invited the grasshopper in to share her warm house and to eat her food for the rest of the winter.

When spring came the following year, grasshopper was right beside the ant. He helped her work the ground and plant the seeds for the next winter. At the end of the day, the grasshopper would dance and sing. He had learned an important lesson; it is always better to work and then play.

Work, Work All Day Long
Said the Little Ant
This Is My Song!

Work, then Play All Day Long
Said the Little Grasshopper
This Is My Song!

Ant Puppet

How To

- Copy the pattern and tape it to a brown piece of art foam (purchase at local craft store).
- Cut out the pattern and add detail lines with black permanent marker.
- Attach the ant to a paint stick or tongue depressor.

Grasshopper Puppet

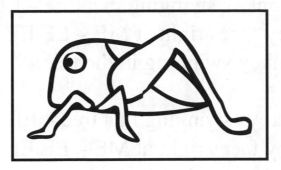

How To
*   Copy the pattern and tape it to a green piece of art foam (purchase at local craft store).
*   Cut out the pattern and add detail lines with black permanent marker.
*   Attach the grasshopper to a paint stick or tongue depressor.

Monkey Business

I saw a little monkey swinging in a tree – EE EE EE EE!
Making monkey faces right at ME – EE EE EE EE!
One funny monkey swinging in the tree.

Two little monkeys swinging in a tree – EE EE EE EE!
Making monkey faces right at ME – EE EE EE EE!
Two funny monkeys swinging in the tree.

Three little monkeys swinging in a tree – EE EE EE EE!
Making monkey faces right at ME – EE EE EE EE!
Three funny monkeys swinging in the tree.

Four little monkeys swinging in a tree – EE EE EE EE!
Making monkey faces right at ME – EE EE EE EE!
Four funny monkeys swinging in the tree.

Five little monkeys swinging in the tree – EE EE EE EE!
Making monkey faces right at ME – EE EE EE EE!
Five funny monkeys swinging in the tree.

Kid Fun

The children can repeat the fun rhyme and make funny monkey faces

Jug Puppets

Creating a puppet from a gallon or half-gallon plastic jug is an economical way to provide many children with a puppet character to accompany a good story. Some jugs contain drinking water, distilled water, milk, juice or unused jugs can be found at a local milk company. Some milk companies will donate jugs for a project. We are helping the Earth by using recyclable materials like the plastic jugs. Children can use their imaginations to create and decorate a puppet. They can tell, retell or write a story to accompany the puppet.

Materials:

- A clean plastic jug - gallon or half-gallon
- Sharp scissors (for adult use only)
- Tape
- Avery markers (These are the markers that work best on the plastic.) They come in many colors and as highlighters. The highlighters give the puppets a brighter color and some will glow in the dark. Purchase these markers at local office supply stores. Crafty Dab paint can also be purchased at local craft stores. This paint is designed to stick to plastic and not crack off.

Make a copy of the original jug pattern and cut out the pattern.

Handle

The handle of the jug is what the children hold onto when using the jug to tell a story, sing a song, or march in a parade or just having fun.

How To

Wash the plastic jug thoroughly and fill the jug with hot water. Let the hot water sit inside the jug for several minutes and then peel off the label. If you have difficulty, try some Goo Gone from your local discount store. Only adults should use this glue remover.

Jug Puppets

Directions for most jugs:

Cut off the small top where the lid screws on (the spout).

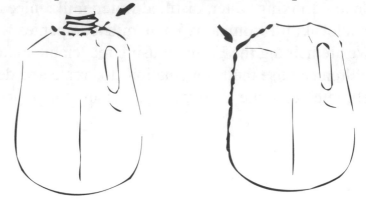

Cut down the middle on the opposite side of the handle to open the jug.

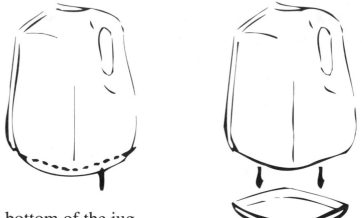

Cut away the bottom of the jug.

Review pattern directions to see if the bottom is needed to create your puppet. A few patterns may need the bottom of the jug for the character.

Tape pattern A to one side of the jug handle and pattern B on the other side of the handle. Patterns should be placed at the top of the jug first. Trace the pattern with a black permanent marker then remove the paper pattern and cut out the puppet on the traced lines.

Or tape pattern A on one side of the jug handle and pattern B on the other side of the handle. Cut around the paper pattern without tracing. Some patterns may have to be adjusted according to the contour of the jug. Use your judgment on the pattern. Decorate the jug puppet to suit your story and add the features such as eyes, mouth, hair, etc.

Summer Surprise © 2003 Monday Morning Books, Inc.

Jug Puppets

When the pattern is on the jug and you see an excess of plastic (plastic outside the pattern line or pattern) cut it away before trying to cut out the puppet. Save your plastic scraps and cut shapes or other items and put in a literacy center or an art center.

Test your jug to see if the marker or paint looks better on the inside or the outside of the jug. Plastic varies from state to state.

Attach a piece of rope to the ceiling of your classroom and attach the jugs to the string with clothespins for storage. A clothes line can also be attached to the walls and jugs attached to this line for storage.

Note: Always complete the pattern at TOP and BOTTOM of the jug where the paper pattern does not meet.

Kid Fun

The children can use the Avery markers or Crafty Dab paint to create a rainbow of colors for their jug puppet. This is a free art experience and hands-on activity that can be repeated throughout the year. The puppets can be sent home or used in a story area at school.

Let the children be creative. There is no right and wrong way to do this project.

Scraps of leftover plastic can be recycled. Cut the leftover plastic in any design; add color with the markers, punch a hole and string the pieces and hang in a window or from the ceiling.

Family Fun

Send your families the instructions and patterns for the puppets. The children and their family members can cut out different kinds of puppets to use with storytelling and story retelling. They can make puppets to represent the members of their family and tell their story. Parents can help the children make puppets and write special stories for the class. This is a great connection between classroom and home.

The Day the Rainbow Fell From the Sky

It was a stormy day and the rainbow knew when the sun began to shine she would begin to show her colors.

It was a bad storm with heavy rain and blowing winds. The rainbow could not hold herself up because the wind was so strong and the rain beat her so hard she collapsed to the ground.

After the storm passed all the animals of the forest _____
(Invite the children to name some forest animals.)
looked at the beautiful colors laying on the forest floor. The animals began playing with the colors.

They danced and raised the colors into the air and watched them float back to the ground *(float colored pieces of tissue paper or use streamers).*

"Help me! Help me! Help me! I need to get back up in the sky or I will die," said the rainbow.

"What can we do?" asked the animals. Some of the animals grabbed the middle and tried to pull it back up in the sky, but it was too heavy and fell back to the ground.

"We will throw it up in the sky," said some of the other animals. "STAND BACK," and they picked up one end of the rainbow. Counting one, two, three they tried to throw it back up in the sky, but it fell back to the ground.

They could not figure out how to help the rainbow get back in the sky before she died.

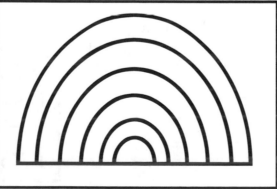

The Day the Rainbow Fell From the Sky

Chameleon was hanging high up in one of the trees and no one noticed her. She was such a drab color that she looked like the bark on the tree itself. She told the birds to grab the ends of the rainbow and fly towards her. She wanted to reach out and grab the rainbow with her strong tail and hold onto it.

The birds began to swoop down and attach themselves to the rainbow. With full force, they began to fly high in the sky towards the chameleon.

The birds began singing a song as they flew towards the chameleon.

Fly, fly, fly in the sky
Fly, fly, fly up high

Raise the rainbow colors bright
Flying, flying with all our might.

The birds flew high enough for the chameleon to grab the middle of the rainbow and hold it up high in the sky. All the animals cheered and the rainbow smiled. She told the chameleon that she would repay her kindness by giving her the colors of the rainbow to wear forever.

Even today the chameleon can change her colors, hanging by her tail and saying Ahhhhh! to a job well done.

Rainbow Jug Puppet

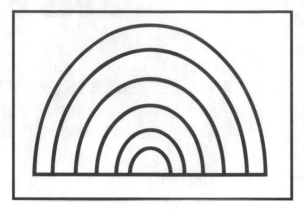

Note: Tape this pattern to the inside of a half-gallon jug. Cut and color. Center over the handle holes. Cut on outside lines only.

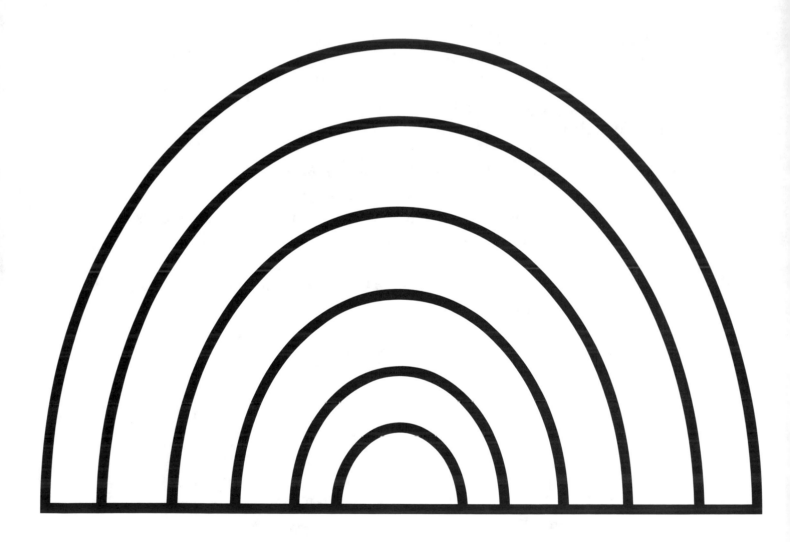

Chameleon Jug Puppet

A

Chameleon Jug Puppet
B

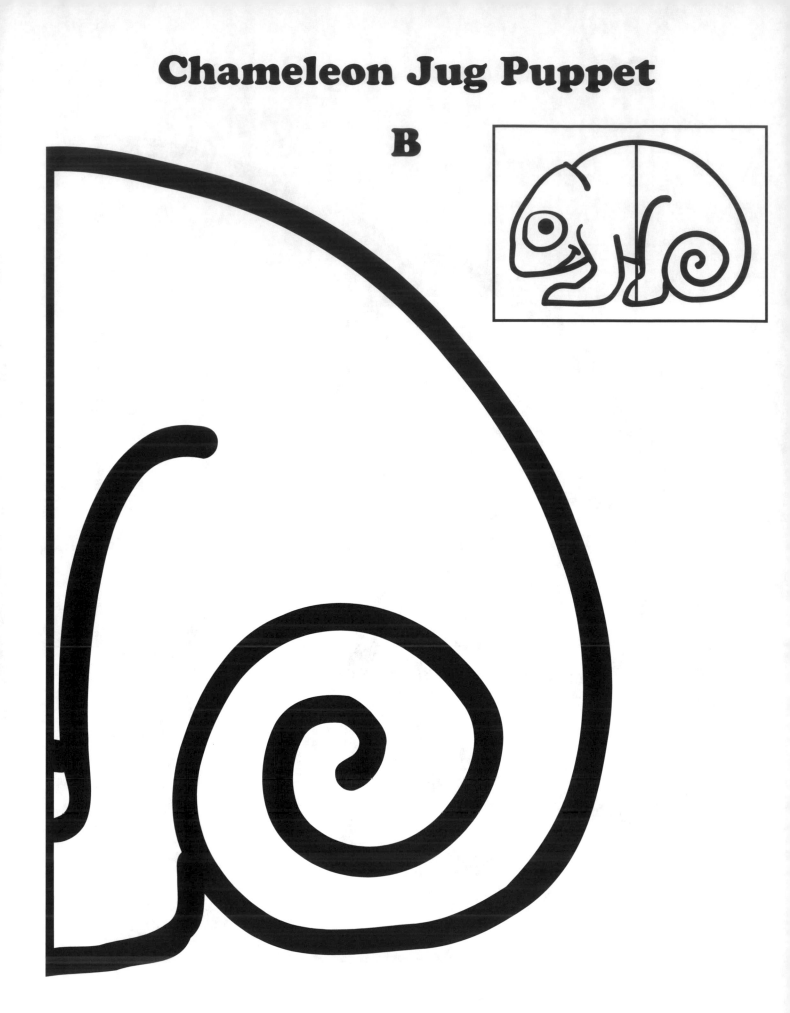

The Lion and the Mouse

Aesop

One day in a time before yesterday, early in the morning at daybreak's edge, a Lion was sleeping soundly. He was awakened by a tiny Mouse running across his body. The Lion roared (Roooaaarrr!) and grabbed the little Mouse with his big paws. "O King of the jungle please do not eat me. I will never forget your kindness if you let me go. Someday I may be able to repay you." The Lion roared with laughter (Haaah! Haaah! Haaah!) and was so amused that the little Mouse thought he could repay him, that he turned the Mouse loose.

Time passed and one day the mighty Lion was caught in a net. The net was laid by clever hunters. The Lion was strong and King of the jungle, but he could not break free from the trap. The forest echoed with loud, angry roars. (Roooaaarrr! Roooaaarrr! Roooaaarrr!)

The tiny Mouse heard the roars and ran to see what the problem was. When he saw the Lion trapped by the big net he began to gnaw at the ropes. He gnawed until the Lion was set free. The lion roared a happy roar. (Roooaaarrr!) "See," said the little Mouse, "I told you I would repay your kindness someday."

Remember: Passing friends may prove to be great friends!

Lion Jug Puppet

A

Punch holes on dots and string yarn through the holes to create a male lion.

Lion Jug Puppet

B

Mouse Jug Puppet

A

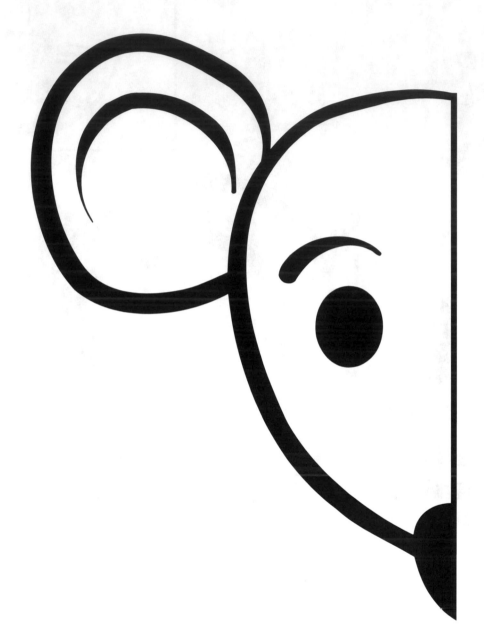

Mouse Jug Puppet

B

Elephant Fun

Use a white sheet and a black marker to create a spider's web. Spread the sheet on the floor and sing the following song. Include all children in the class.

Make a jug puppet for each child and let them color the elephants with markers.

One elephant went out to play
Out on a spider's web one day
He asked another elephant to come
Because he was having so much fun.

Two elephants went out to play
Out on a spider's web one day
They asked another elephant to come
Because they were having so much fun.

Three elephants went out to play
Out on a spider's web one day
They asked another elephant to come
Because they were having so much fun.

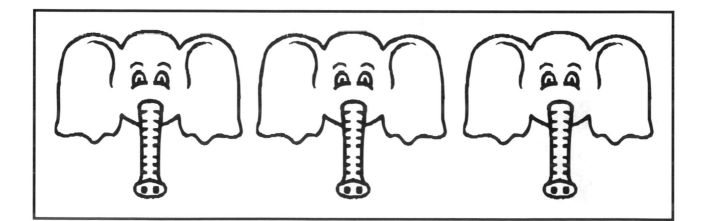

   Summer Surprise © 2003 Monday Morning Books, Inc.

Elephant Fun

Continue the rhyme until you have all the children in the class on the web. They will all be having fun!

The jug puppet on the following page can be used by the children in the class. Designate a particular number (such as five elephants) if the whole class will not be participating.

Note: The elephant jug puppet requires the bottom of the jug. DO NOT cut out the bottom. Tape the pattern on the whole jug and then cut only on the traced lines. This jug puppet is an exception to the regular directions.

This pattern is in three pieces and the trunk should be taped to the jug to line up with the ears. The trunk uses part of the bottom and front of the jug. After cutting, bend the trunk back so it hangs down.

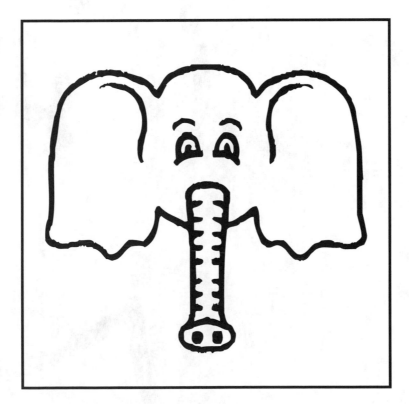

El phant Jug Puppet

A

Elephant Jug Puppet
B

Elephant Jug Puppet

Note: This pattern is taped to the jug and uses part of the front and bottom.

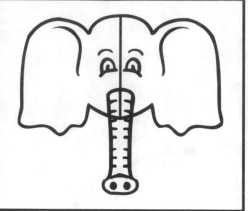

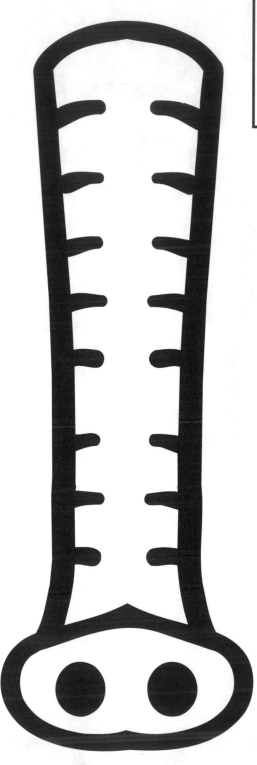

Fishy

Fishy, fishy in the sea
Fishy, fishy swimming by me.

Fishy one is on the run
Wanting to play and have some fun.

Fishy two is hiding away
Waiting for someone to come and play.

Fishy three circles around
Quiet, quiet without a sound

Fishy one,
Fishy two,
Fishy three,
How many fishes do you see?

Fish Jug Puppet

A

Make three fish to interact with this rhyme.

Fish Jug Puppet
B

Ollie, Ollie, Octopus

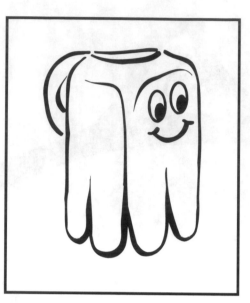

Ollie, Ollie Octopus
On the ocean floor.
Moving here and moving there
Eight legs waving everywhere.

Ollie, Ollie Octopus
On the ocean floor.
Be my friend and share with me
How to count past four.

Ollie, Ollie Octopus
On the ocean floor.
Be my friend and teach me well
Or I will hide inside my shell.

One, two, three, four
Five, six, seven, eight
Thank you Ollie for helping me.
A mathematician I can be.

Kid Fun

The children use a snail puppet to ask the octopus to help them count. Snail can also teach the children the rhyme. Use this before a math activity because the children will call themselves mathematicians.

Octopus Jug Puppet

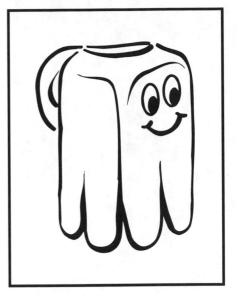

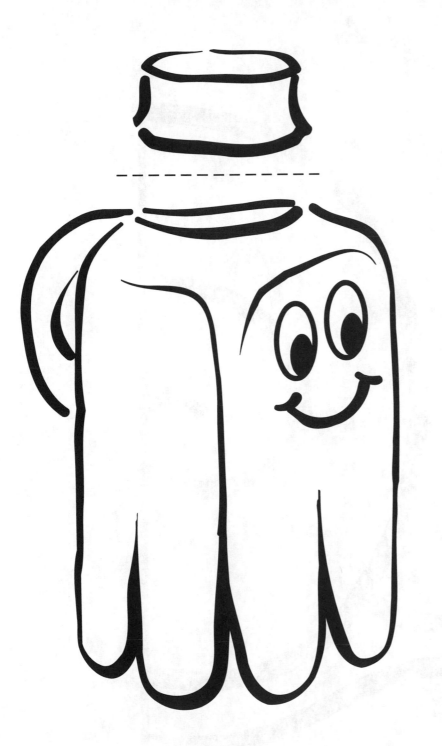

Note: This puppet uses a half-gallon plastic jug. Cut out the top neck and the bottom of the jug. DO NOT cut the jug down the side. Two legs are drawn on each panel of the jug. Cut out two legs on each side of the jug. Add eyes with a marker or glue on big wiggle eyes. Put numbers on the legs so the children can count.

Snail Jug Puppet
A

Snail Jug Puppet
B

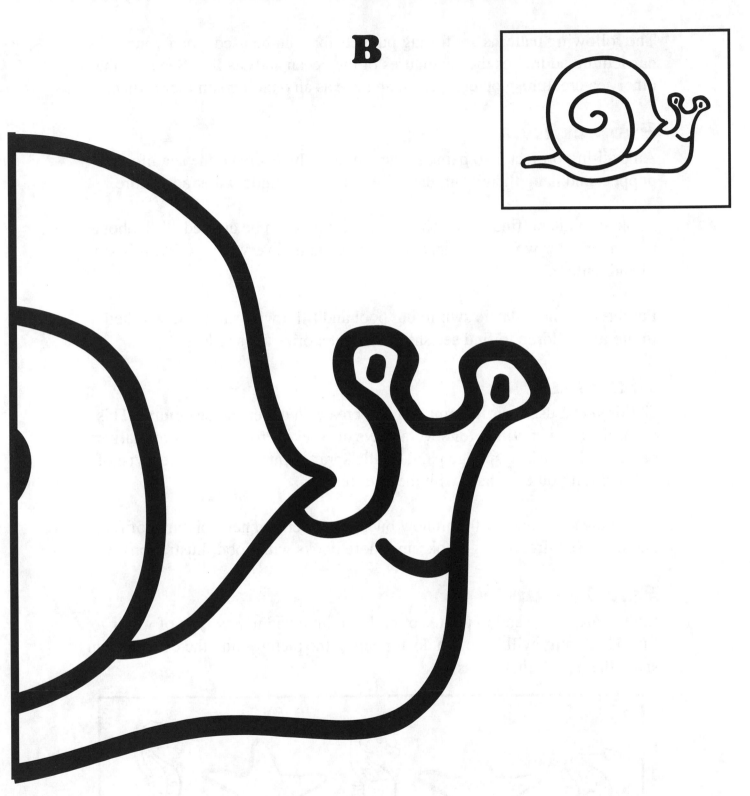

Jug Puppet Special

The following patterns are for jug puppets that can be used when your curriculum addresses the adventures of the ocean and sea life. See how many other sea creatures you can design and use as an ongoing summer project.

Project Idea

An exciting project is to paint all the windows blue, create the sea life jug puppets and hang them from the ceiling to feel an underwater adventure.

Look around and find areas where sea life caves can be created. Talk about the underwater world and add a different creature every day during this sea life adventure.

Purchase a small plastic swimming pool and fill it with sand and sea shells. Invite the children to find sea shells and categorize the shells.

Kid Fun

Children can use their imagination and create an under-the-sea mural. This art project can continue for several days or weeks. Provide types of markers, paints with brushes, sponge paint, bottle spray paints and any other type of art medium you can share with the children.

Set up the story area with minnow buckets, fisherman nets, pictures of fish and other sea life, books, books and more books with good illustrations.

Family Fun

Invite parents to send in photos of children involved in any type of water fun. The family will have fun documenting the pictures and the children can share them with their class.

Sea Horse Jug Puppet

Note: Tape this pattern to the inside of a half-gallon jug. Cut and color. Center over the handle holes.

Starfish Jug Puppet

Note: Tape this pattern to the inside of a half-gallon jug. Cut and color. Center over the handle holes. Glue sand on the starfish to give it texture.

Crab Jug Puppet

A

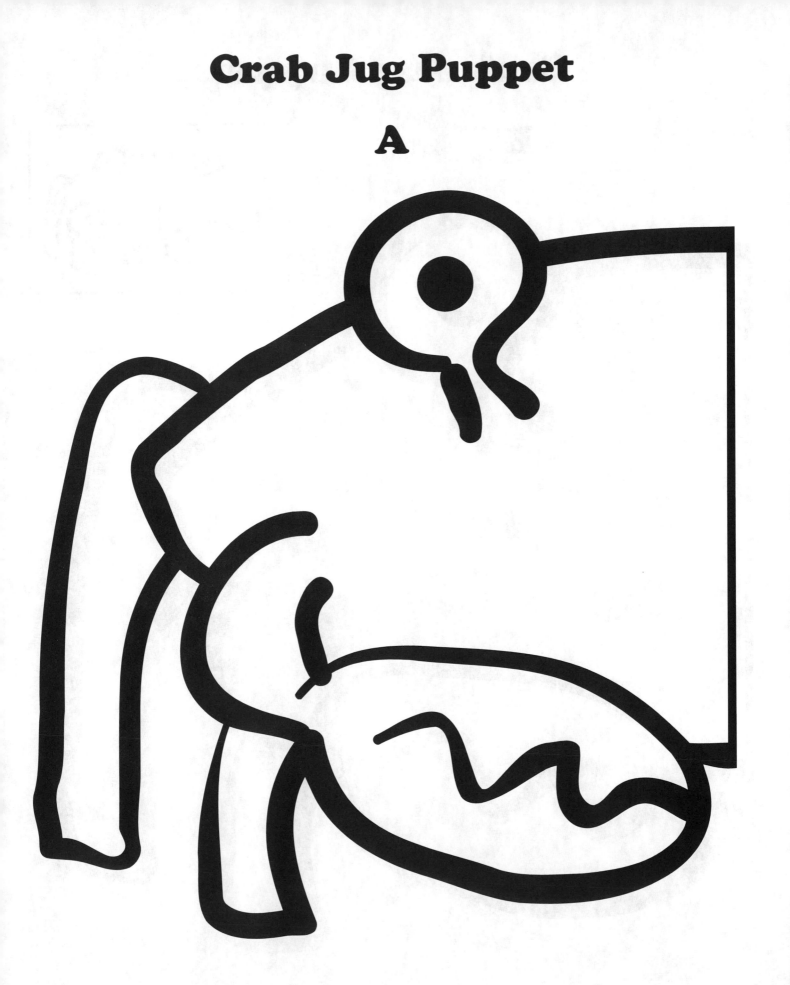

Crab Jug Puppet
B

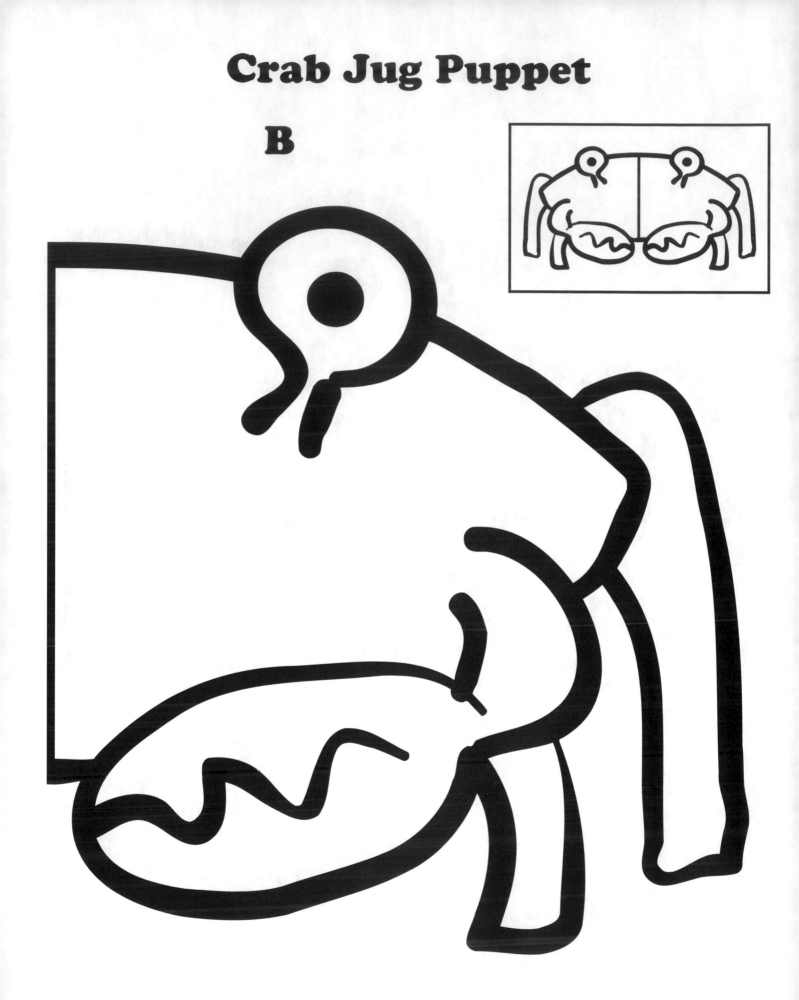

Whale Jug Puppet

A

Whale Jug Puppet
B

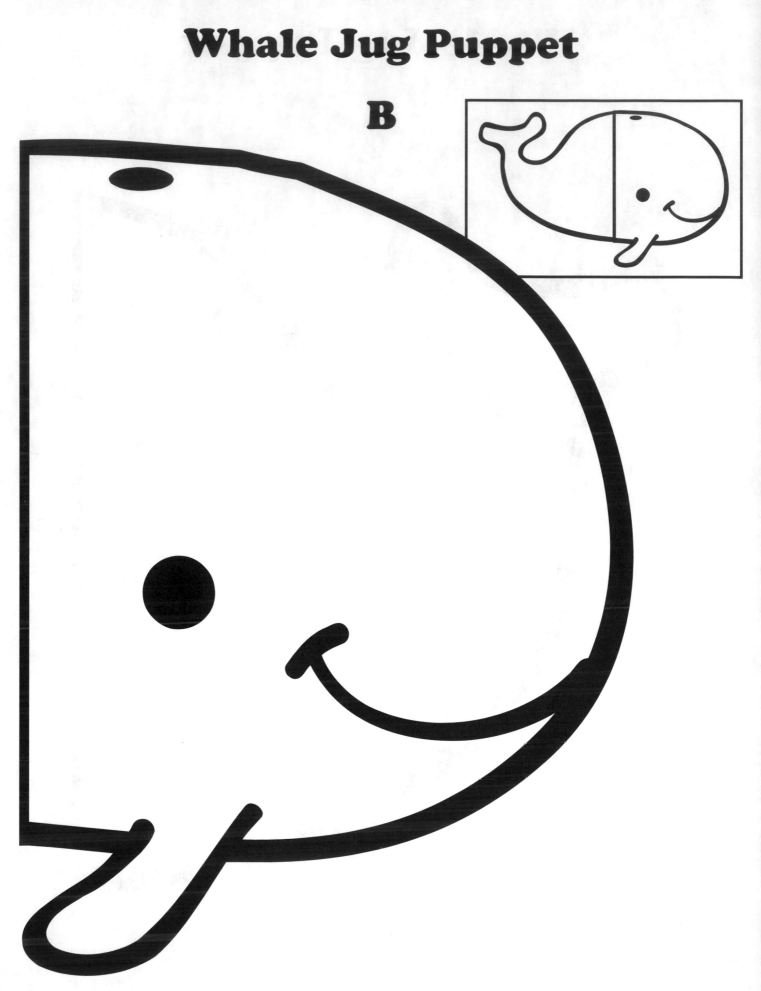

Summer Surprise © 2003 Monday Morning Books, Inc.

Jellyfish Jug Puppet

Note: Tape the pattern on the inside of the jug and center over handle holes.
Use a hole punch around the bottom of the jug and attach colorful ribbons.

Summer Tales

Allen, Judy, *Are You a Snail?* (Kingfisher, 2000)

Andreae, Giles, *Commotion in the Ocean* (Scholastic, 1999)

Galloway, Ruth, *Fidgety Fish* (Scholastic, 2001)

Randall, Ronne, *Gym Giraffe* (Bright Sparks Press, 2000)

Pfister, Marcus, *How Leo Learned to Be King* (Scholastic, 1998)

Kraus, Robert, *Leo the Late Bloomer* (Scholastic, 1971)

Van Laan, Nancy, *Little Fish, Lost* (Atheneum Books, 1998)

Randall, Ronne, *Monkey Mayhem* (Bright Sparks Press, 2000)

Dubrovin, Vivian, *Storytelling For the Fun of It* (Storycraft Publishing, 1999)

Kleven, Elisa, *The Lion and the Little Red Bird* (Dutton Press, 1992)

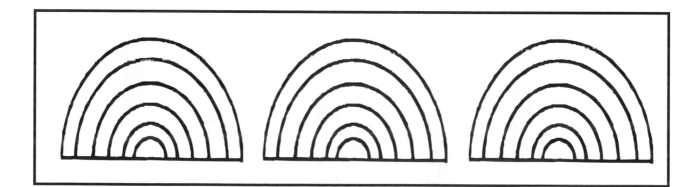

Summer Tales

Andreae, Giles, *The Lion Who Wanted to Love* (Little Tiger Press, 1999)

Pfister, Marcus, *The Rainbow Fish* (Scholastic, 1993)

Hall, Zoe, *The Surprise Garden* (The Blue Sky Press, 1998)

Randall, Ronne, *Trunk Trouble* (Bright Sparks Press, 2000)

Baker, Jeannie, *Where the Forest Meets the Sea* (Greenwillow, 1987)

National Storytelling Network and other web sites

www.storynet.org
www.youthstorytelling.org
www.storytellin.com
www.rivertownstorytellers.com
www.meddybemps.com
www.ms_creations.com

Storytelling Resources

Mary Jo Huff, the author of many books from
Monday Morning is available for
Keynotes, Workshops, Storytelling Presentations,
and Family Nights.
Contact her at 800-213-0527
E-mail: mjohuff@att.net
www.storytellin.com

Resources available at www.storytellin.com

"Loop"–The Velcro compatible material
"Hook"–Used for all storytelling items on the Loop material
Storytelling Apron–Velcro type material for storytelling
Story Bands–Storytelling tool for "Kid Fun"
Used for dramatic play
Commercial "Peepers"–Great language tool for retelling stories
Peeper Power–Learn how to use Peepers
Storyboard Felt Story Characters & CD
"Varmint"–Mr. Mascot and other puppet friends
CDs written & recorded by Mary Jo Huff

Jerry Jindrich, the illustrator of this book,
is the master of a special web site.
www.meddybemps.com

This free web site is for teachers, young children
and their parents. You can read, play and learn at
this popular site. Meddybemps.com is great fun,
written and illustrated in Jerry's incomparable
style, accessible via the internet and the best of all,
it's free!